MY LITTLE BRAIN!

Explaining The Human Brain for Kids

BABY PROFESSOR

EDUCATION KIDS

Speedy Publishing LLC
40 E. Main St. #1156
Newark, DE 19711
www.speedypublishing.com

LEARN ABOUT YOUR

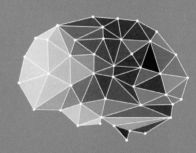

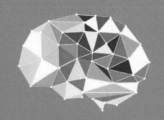

BRAIN

The human brain is like a computer, but a hundred times more powerful. It stores our memory with unlimited capacity. Your brain is the boss of your body. It runs the show and controls just about everything you do.

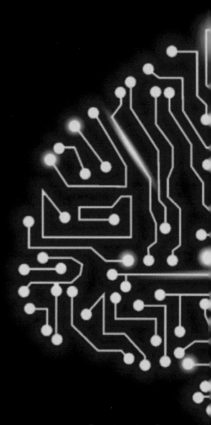

0110
0100
1001

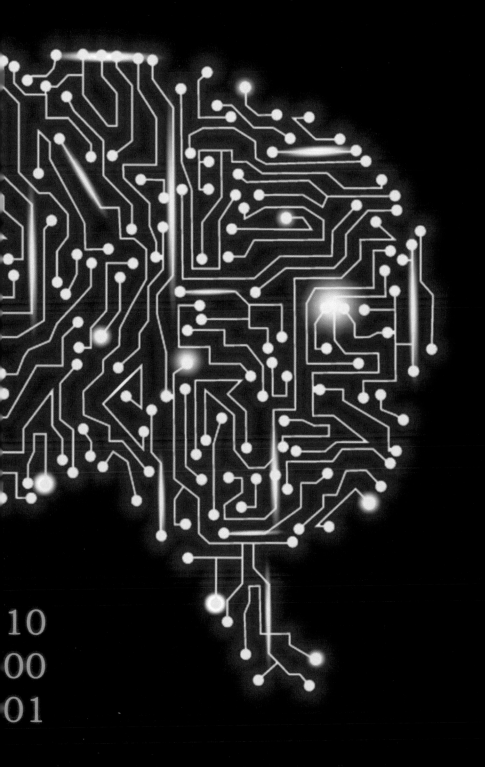

10
00
01

Your amazing brain controls every move you make and how you react. It controls you even when you're asleep. It allows you to feel emotions like happiness, sorrow, and anger.

The brain is a powerful master control panel. The brain sends the signals that make your heart beat, your lungs draw in breath and your eyelids blink. It makes us alive.

The three pound pink, wrinkly mass in your head might not look like much, but it has immense power, capacity and complexity that we still have not completely explored. It has evolved over time and features some incredibly intricate parts that have left scientists baffled for years.

The brain is the center of the human nervous system. There are different parts of the brain that perform particular functions. It sits in your skull at the top of your spinal cord.

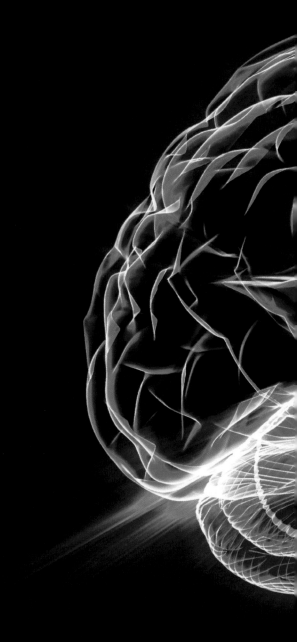

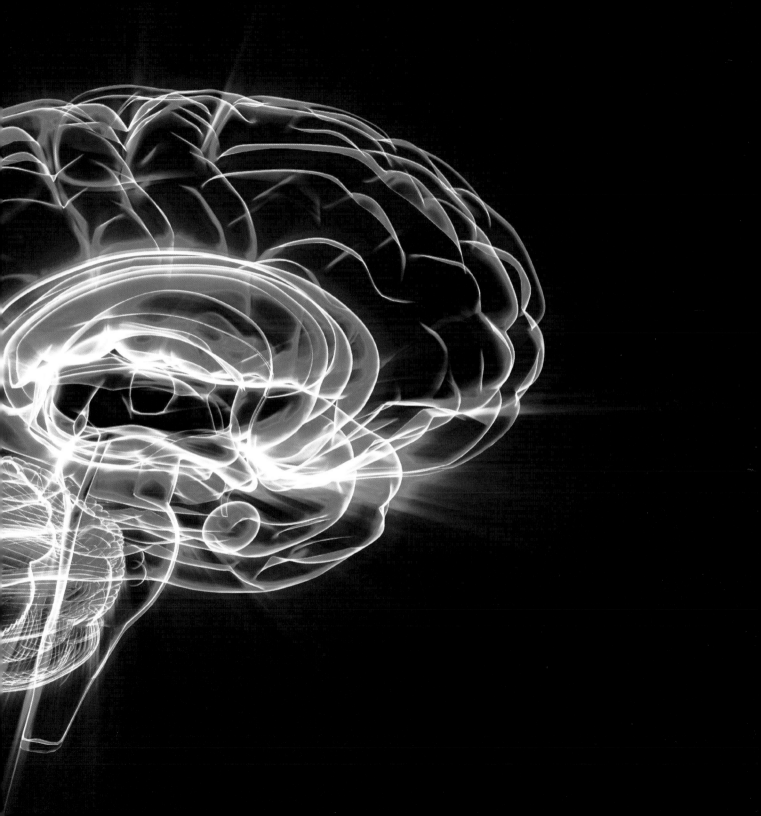

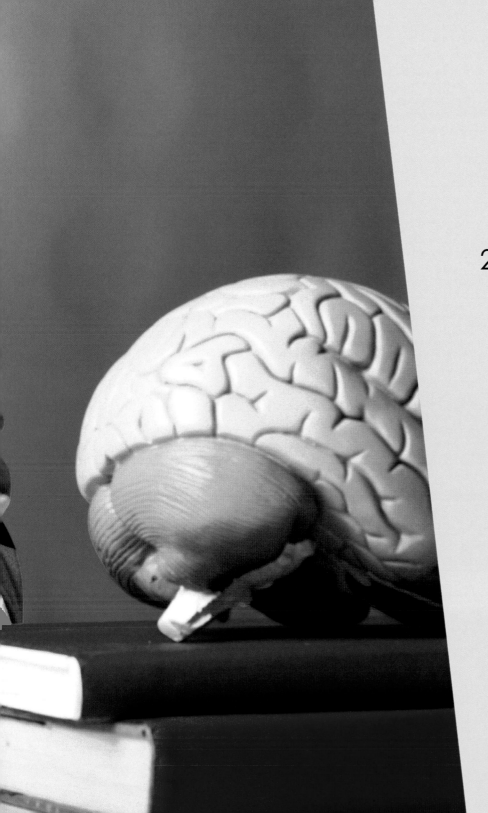

The brain is just 2% of your body weight. It uses around 20% of all your energy from the blood and oxygen in your body. That's a lot for such a small organ.

Your brain stops growing around age 18. It continues to work and develop and learn new things. That is why our parents are smart and why we become smarter as we grow up.

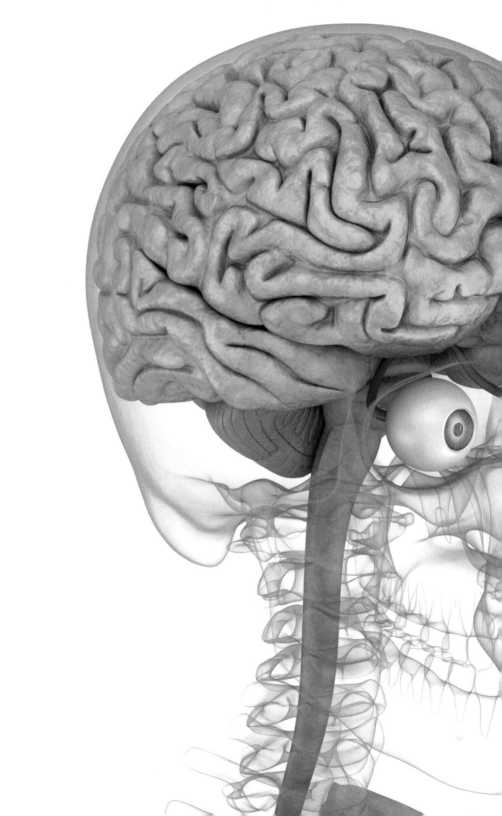

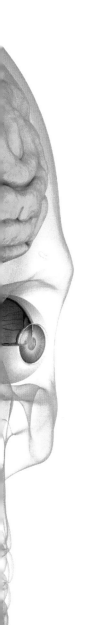

The brain of an adult human weighs around 3 pounds. The brain of an elephant is much larger than a human brain. Our brains are three times bigger than that of a chimpanzee.

The brain of an elephant only makes up 0.15% of their overall weight. When you compare it to our brains, which take up 2% of our body weight, humans still have the largest brain to body size. we're have the most brain power in relation to our size of any creature on Earth.

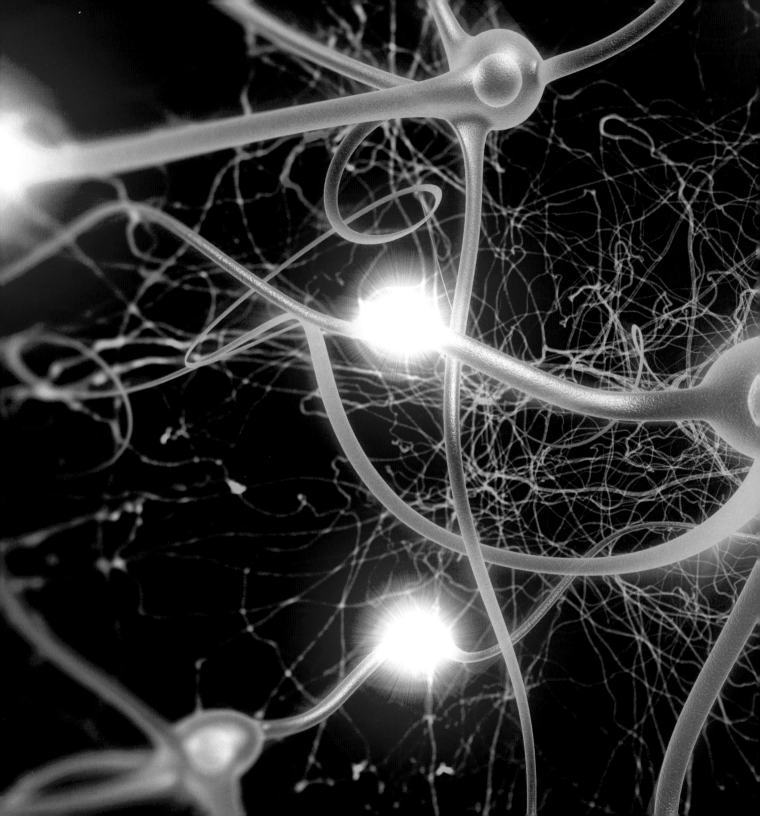

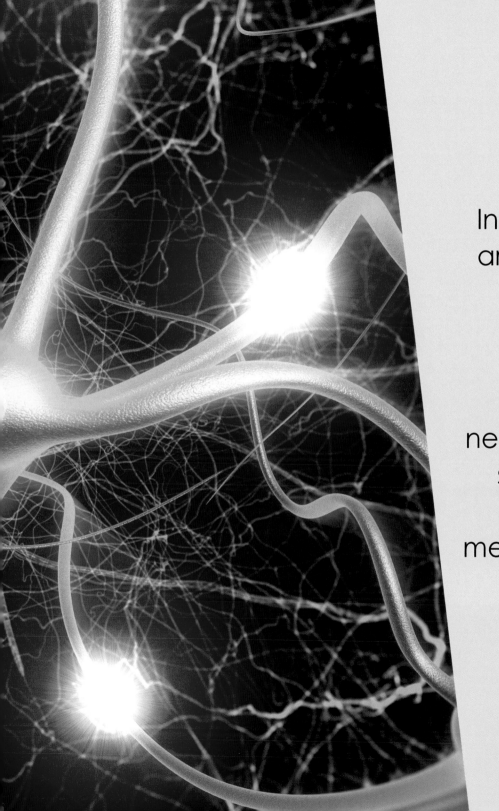

Inside your brain are microscopic cells called neurons. There are about 100 billion tiny, tiny neurons. Neurons send electrical and chemical messages to your body.

Neurons in your brain tell everything what to do. The neurons in one brain send more messages than all the phones in the entire world. They send information to your brain and carry messages from your brain to your body. Your brain never stops working.

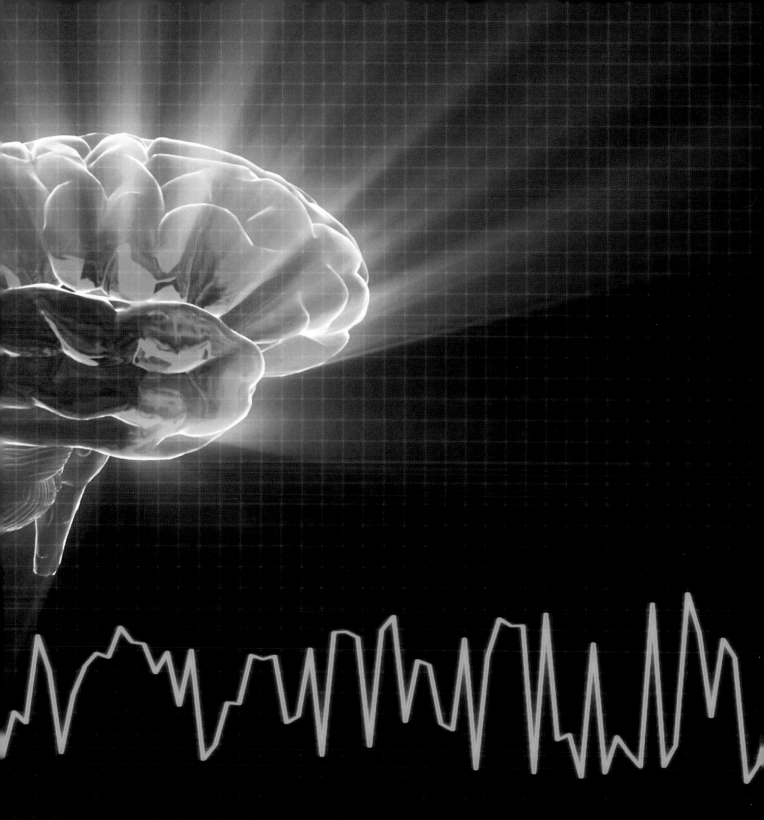

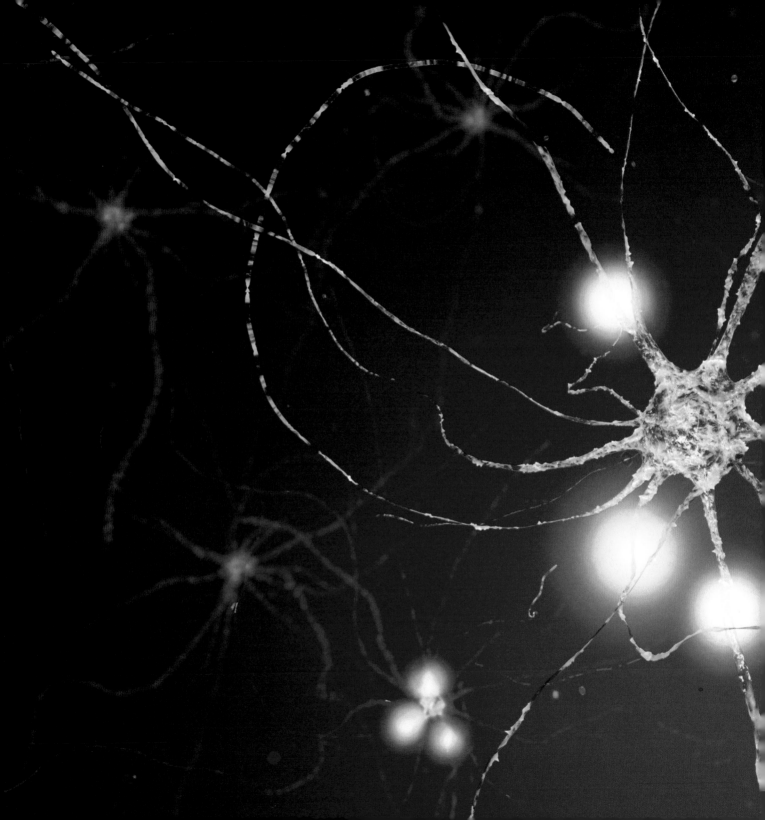

The neurons in your brain create enough electricity to provide power for a low-watt light bulb. Your neurons are connected by tiny pathways. Exercise can make you smarter because it increases the blood flow in the brain.

Your brain has three main parts. The three parts work together. They are the cerebellum, cerebrum, and brain stem.

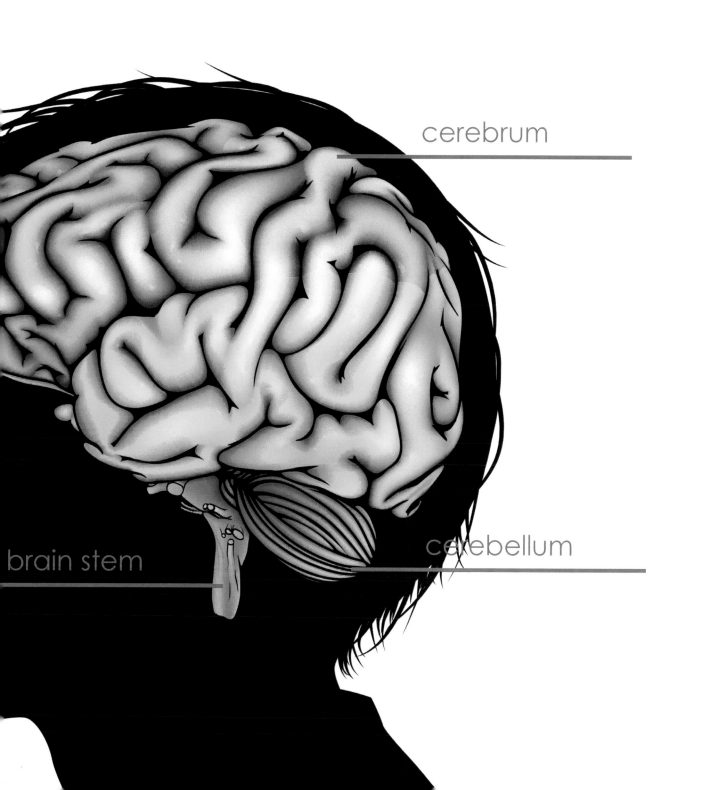

cerebrum

cerebellum

brain stem

The biggest part of the brain is the cerebrum (se-re-brum). The cerebrum makes up 85% of the brain's weight. It is the thinking part of the brain and it controls your voluntary muscles.

The cerebrum is divided into two halves. The right half helps you think like music, colors, and shapes. The left half tends to be more analytical, helping you with math, logic, and speech. The right side of the cerebrum controls the left side of your body, and the left side controls the right.

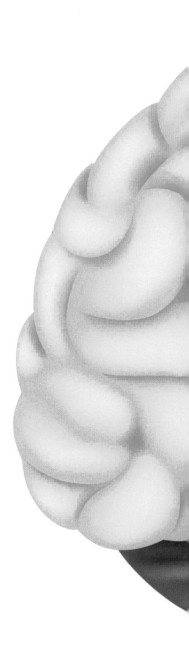

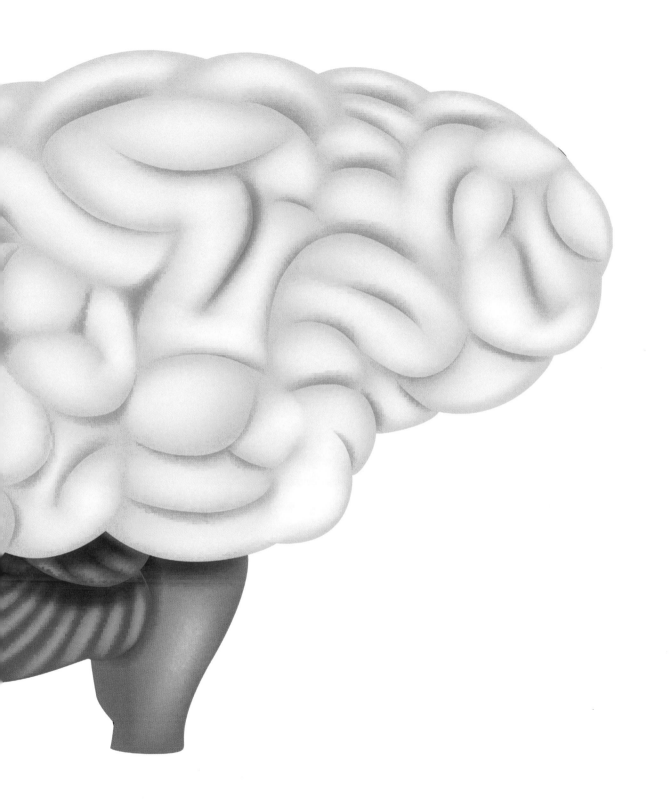

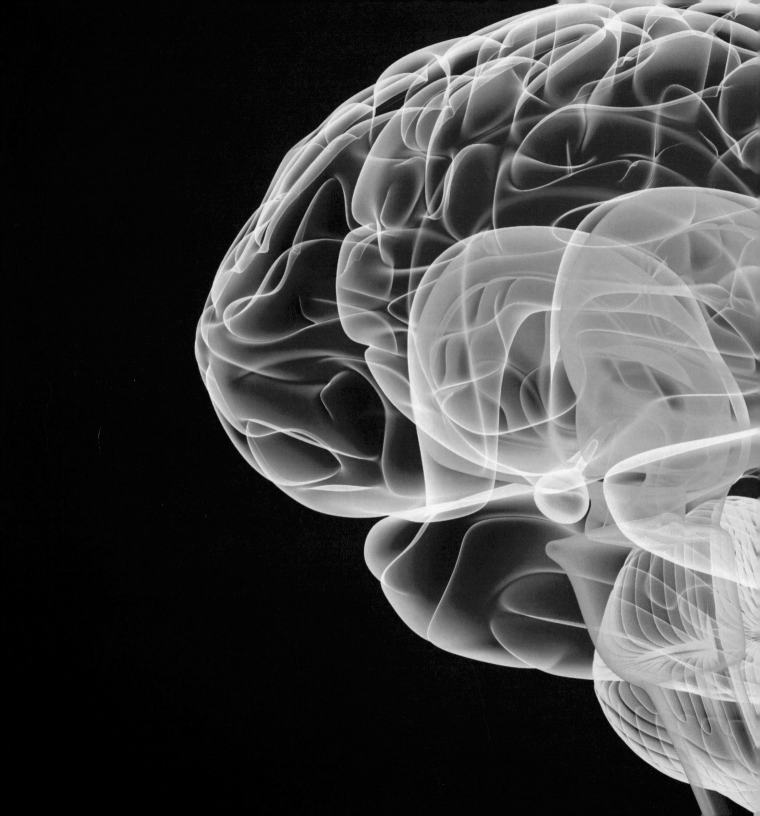

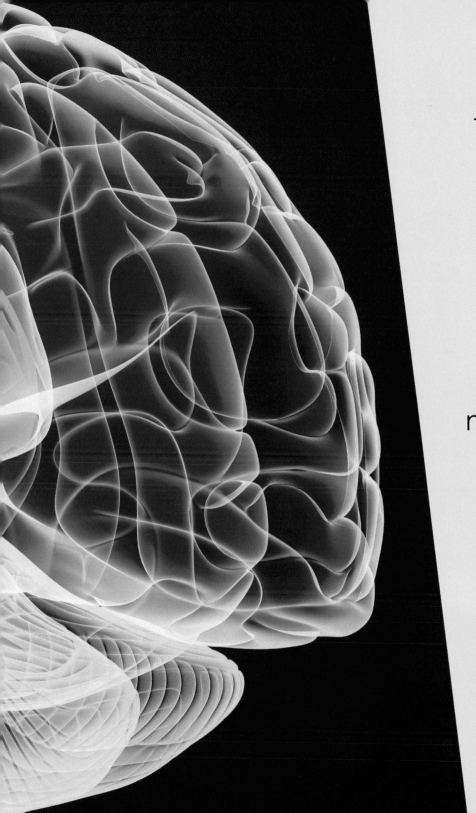

The cerebellum (se-re-bell-um) is located at the back of the brain. The cerebellum controls balance, movement, and coordination. It gives you the ability to stand upright, ride on your bike or cruise on your skateboard.

The brain stem is a small part of the brain, but it is mighty. It connects your brain to your spinal cord and controls many automatic processes in your body. It is in charge of all the functions your body performs to stay alive, like breathing air, digesting food, and circulating blood.

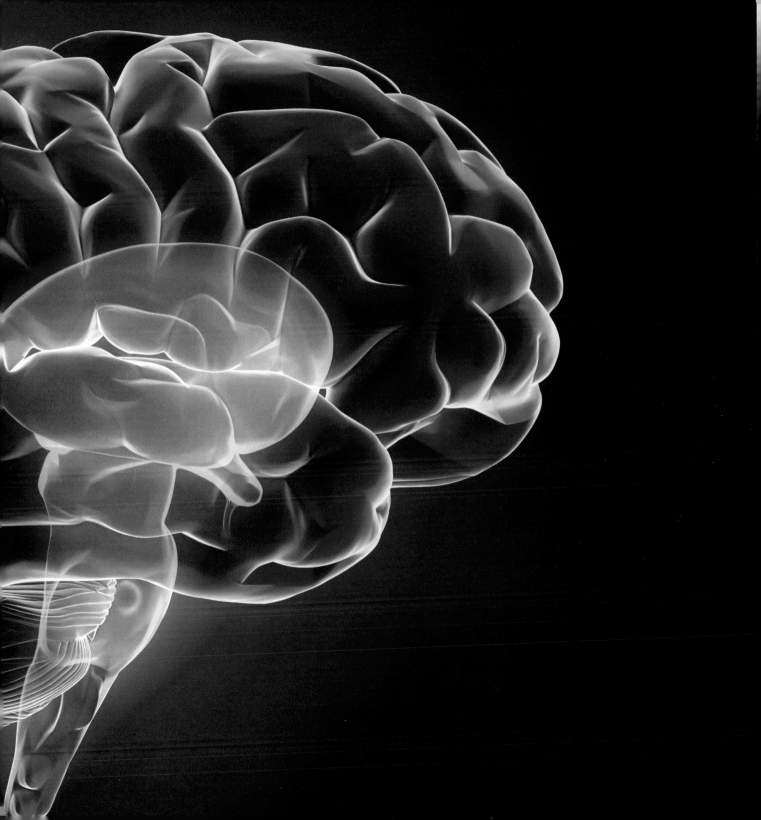

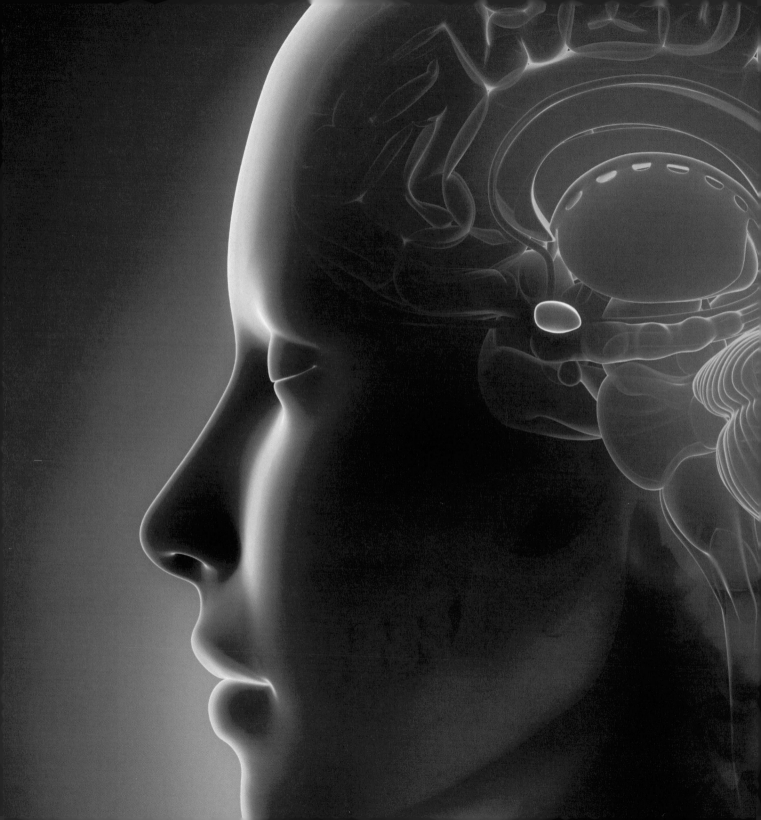

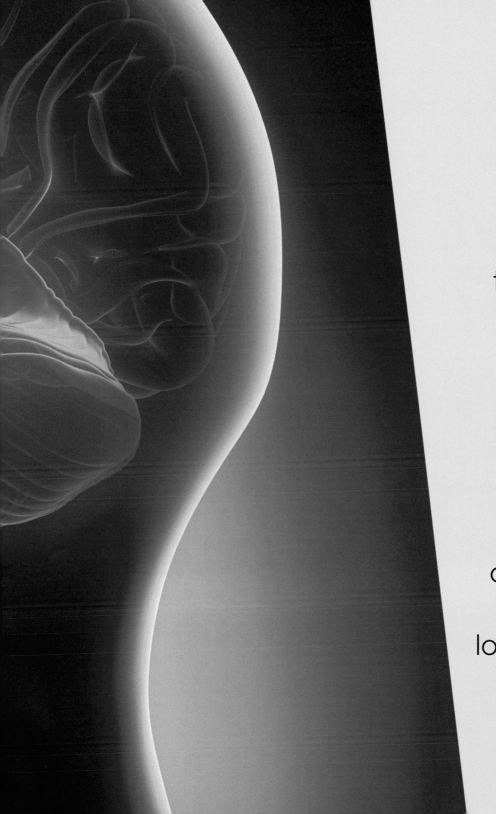

There's a little area in the brain called the amygdala. The amygdala is an almond-shaped group of neurons. It helps us to understand how people and events are feeling by just looking at them.

The pituitary
gland is very
small; it is only
about the
size of a pea.
It plays an
important role,
as it produces
and releases
hormones into
your body which
are the body's
chemical
messengers.

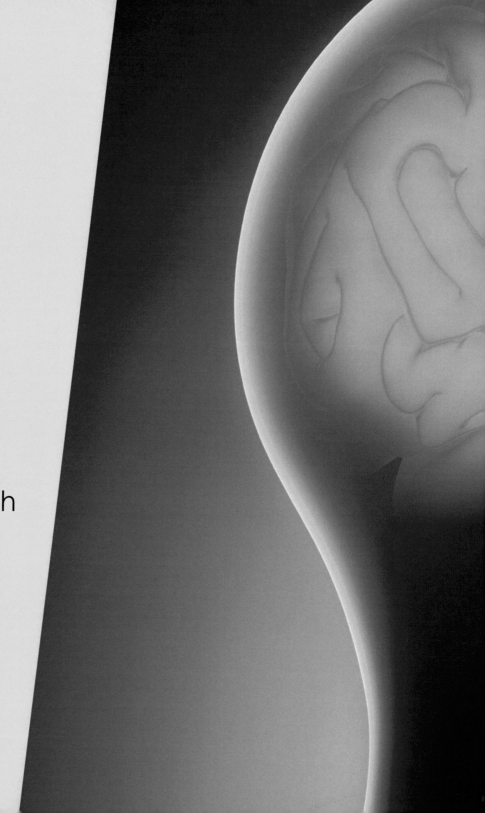

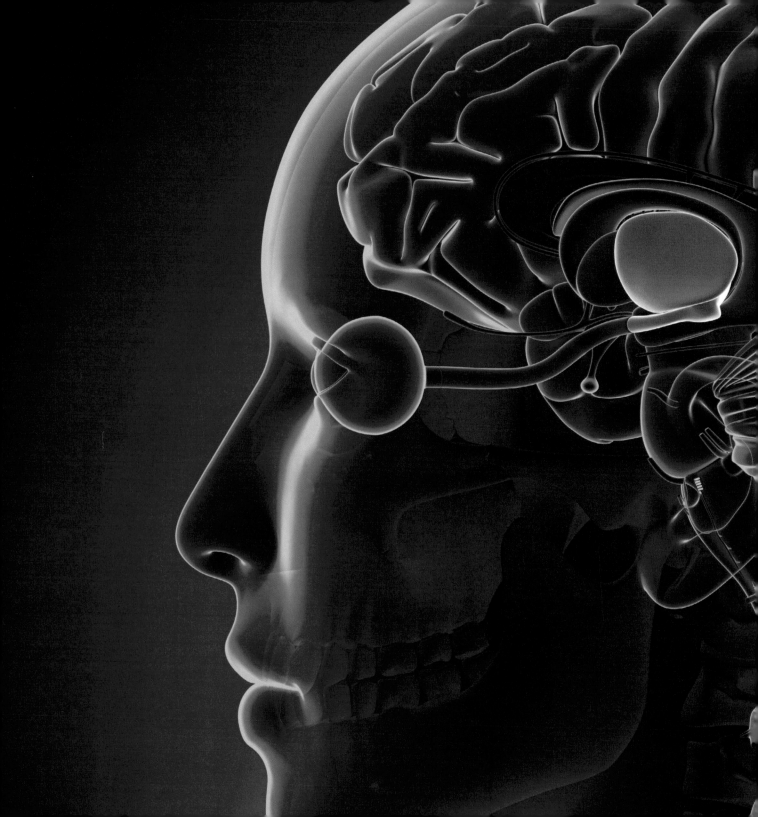

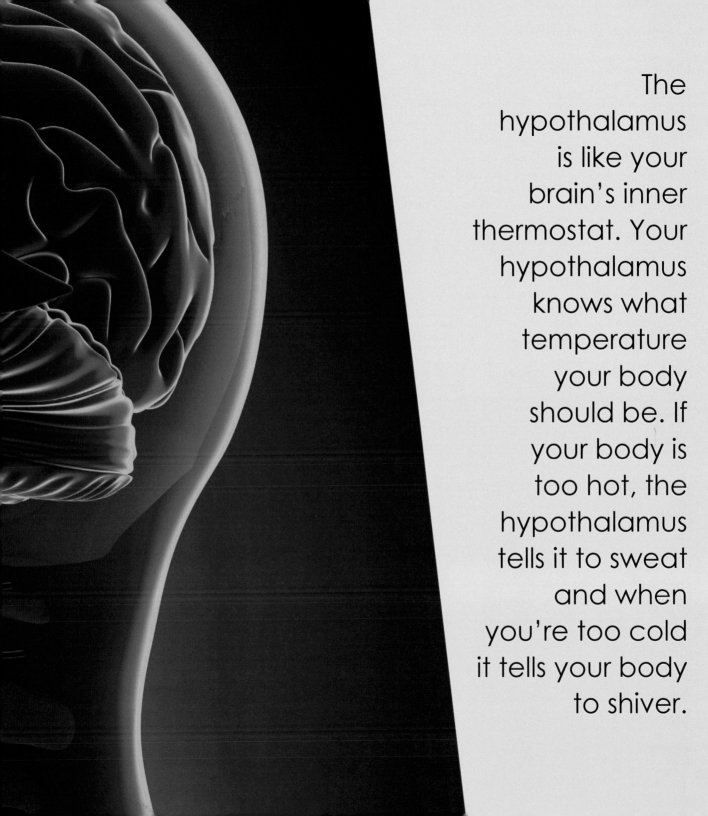

The hypothalamus is like your brain's inner thermostat. Your hypothalamus knows what temperature your body should be. If your body is too hot, the hypothalamus tells it to sweat and when you're too cold it tells your body to shiver.

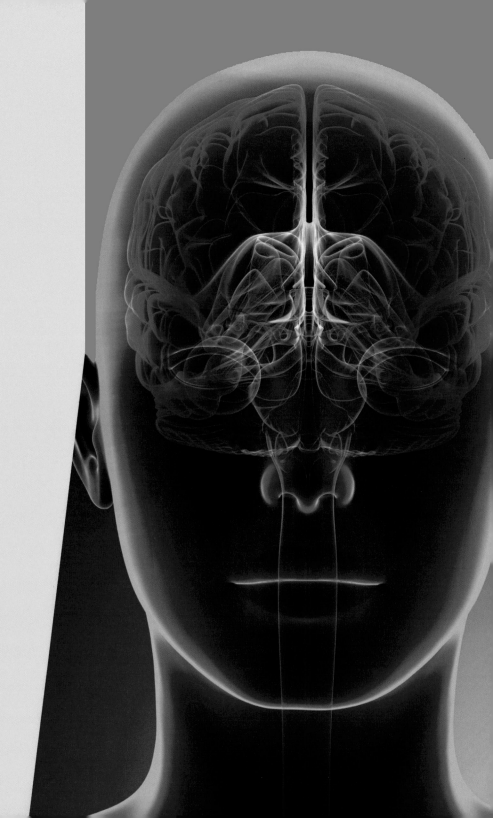

The corpus callosum is the band of white fibers that connects the cerebral hemispheres of your brain. It is right in the middle of your brain. It is also responsible for transmitting messages between the right and left sides of the brain.

The brain is about 60% fat. It's a chubby little organ. The brain is protected by the skull, which is made up of 22 bones that are all joined together.

Cranial nerves carry messages to and from the ears, eyes, nose, throat, tongue and skin on your face and scalp. There are 12 pairs of cranial nerves.

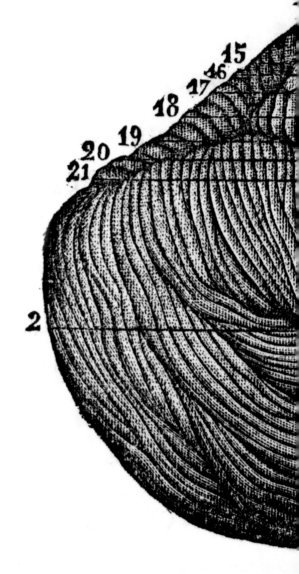

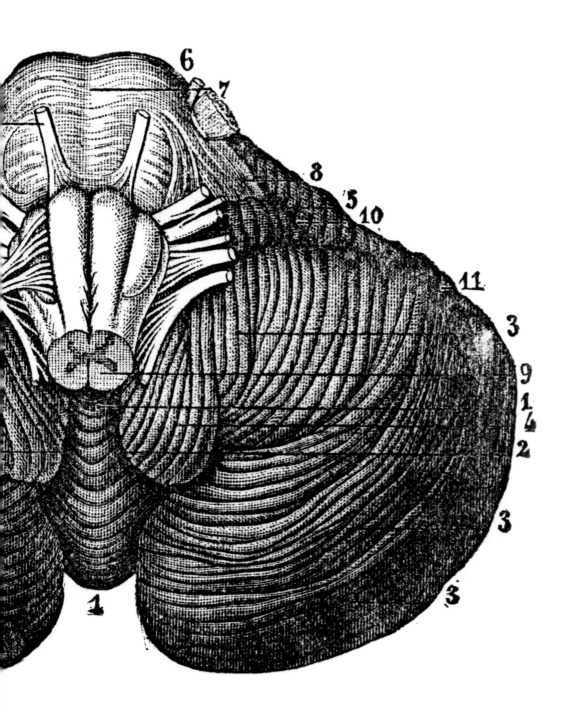

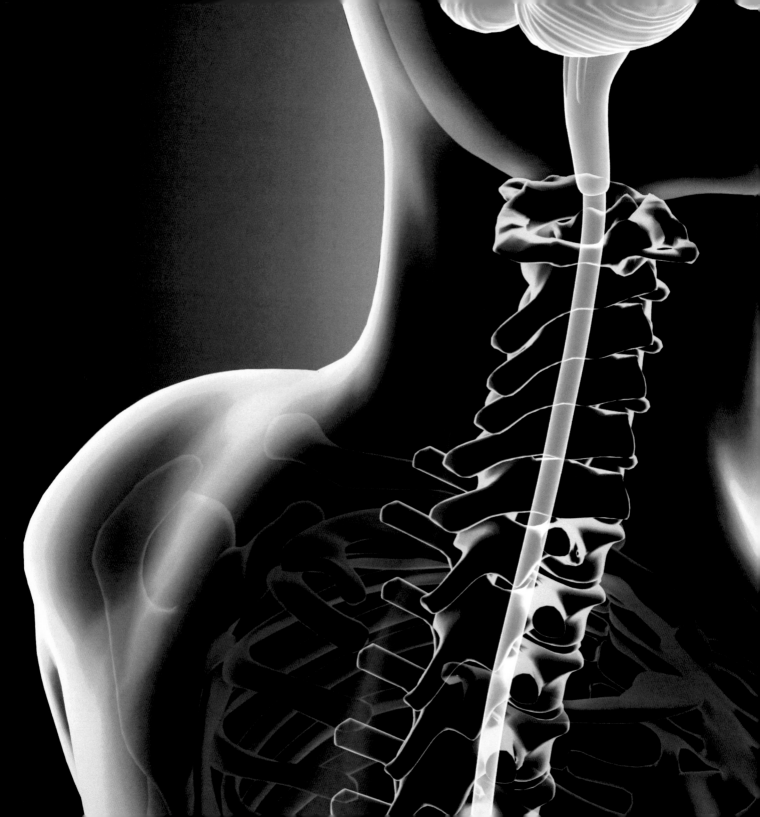

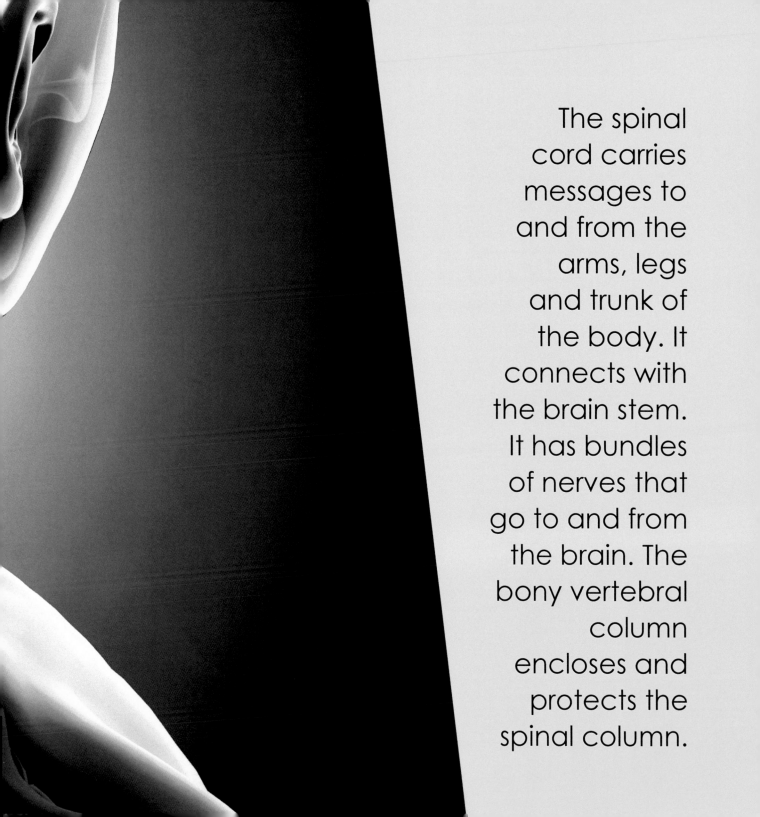

The spinal cord carries messages to and from the arms, legs and trunk of the body. It connects with the brain stem. It has bundles of nerves that go to and from the brain. The bony vertebral column encloses and protects the spinal column.

Did you know
that when a
baby is born,
their brain is
almost the same
size as an adult
brain? At age 6
it reaches its full
size.

Potassium and calcium are the two minerals important for the nervous system. You must eat plenty of healthy foods to keep your brain healthy.

Do challenging activities, such as puzzles, reading, playing music, making art, or anything else that gives your brain a workout. This way you can use your brain and keeps it working well.

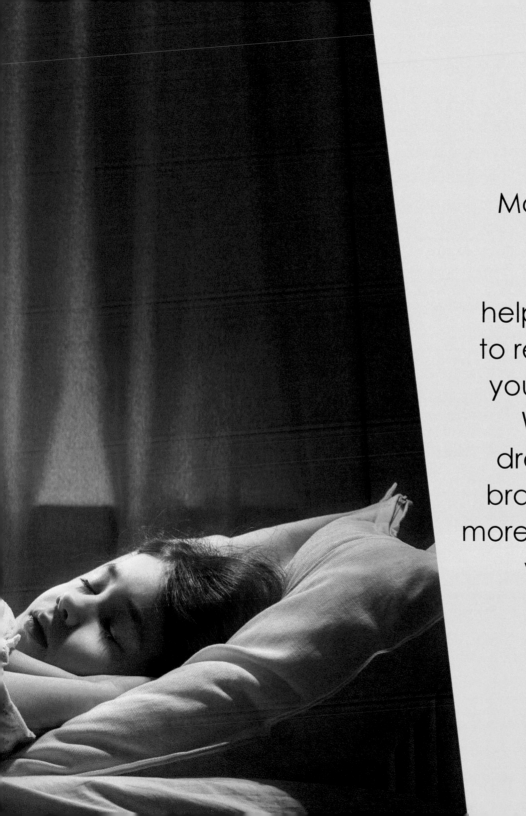

Make sure you get enough sleep. Sleep helps your brain to remember all your memories. When you're dreaming your brainwaves are more active than when you're awake.

Visit

BABY PROFESSOR
EDUCATION KIDS

www.BabyProfessorBooks.com

to download Free Baby Professor eBooks
and view our catalog of new and exciting
Children's Books

Made in the USA
Columbia, SC
06 October 2020